The Nightingales

A comedy

Peter Quilter

Samuel French — London
www.samuelfrench-london.co.uk

Please see page iv for further copyright information.

THE NIGHTINGALES

First performed at the Contra Kreis Theater, Bonn, Germany, on 15th December 2011 with the following cast:

Jack	Leon van Leeuwenberg
Maggie	Elisabeth Ebner
Charlie	Jasper Vogt
Beatrice	Naëmi Priegel
Graham	Thomas Pohn

Translated and directed by Horst Johanning

The character of Graham was changed to Geraldine for the version of the play published here.

CHARACTERS

Jack, 40s/50s
Maggie, 40s/50s
Charlie, Jack's father, 60s/70s
Beatrice, Jack's mother, 60s/70s
Geraldine, 30s/40s

SYNOPSIS OF SCENES

The action of the play takes place in the living-room of Jack's house in the English countryside, not far from London.

ACT I, Scene 1   Morning
ACT I, Scene 2   A day later. The middle of the night
ACT II, Scene 1   Immediately following
ACT II, Scene 2   The following morning

Time — Mid 1950s

A NOTE FROM THE AUTHOR
ABOUT PIANO SEQUENCES

There are three moments in the play when the characters Beatrice and Jack play a bit of piano. It is suggested that the piano playing is pre-recorded and played from hidden speakers placed near to the piano on stage. The actors can then mime the piano playing. Of course, if the actor cast happens to play piano, this will not be necessary, but companies should not restrict their casting by seeking only piano-playing performers. The miming to a recorded track should work perfectly well.

Other plays by Peter Quilter
published by Samuel French Ltd:

BoyBand
The Canterville Ghost
Curtain Up!
Duets
Glorious!

DEDICATION

Peter Quilter would like to dedicate this play to:

Paul Taylor
of Samuel French Ltd (now retired, more or less)
for his advice, assistance and kindness

and
Dawn and Colin Crosby
for their enthusiasm at being my aunty and uncle
(a job that nobody else applied for)

and to
Oscar and Molly
for the unconditional love

ACT I

Scene 1

A living-room in a house in the English countryside, not far from London. Mid 1950s. Morning

A piano. Various armchairs, sofas, tables. A drinks cabinet, a smaller cabinet, telephone, a coat stand, a corner lamp, another lamp and a radio. Two doors at L leading to the bedrooms and the kitchen. Door at R leading to the bathroom. UC is the door leading outside and into the garden/driveway. Maggie's fur coat hangs on a hook next to it

Music plays — a song of the 1950s period — Garland, Astaire, Coward, Sinatra, etc. Maggie sits on the sofa. She is drinking tea and by her side is a solitary but large chocolate biscuit on a plate. A table at L holds cups, plates, milk, sugar, an empty biscuit jar and a pot of tea. The music fades out

Jack enters from the bedrooms, wearing a colourful silk dressing gown

Jack Maggie?
Maggie Morning.
Jack This is unexpected.
Maggie Not as unexpected as your dressing gown. Are those colours legal?
Jack It was a gift.
Maggie I should bloody well hope so.
Jack I thought you were coming at ten.
Maggie I did.
Jack Oh.

Jack looks at his watch. It is indeed 10 a.m.

Maggie Geraldine made some tea and found me a biscuit.
Jack What sort of biscuit?
Maggie Chocolate.
Jack Damn that woman! She can consider herself fired. Those are for guests!

Maggie seeks an explanation

You don't count because you're virtually family. (*He fetches himself a cup of tea*)

Maggie I certainly am not ... Unless of course you plan to marry me?

Jack Don't try that trick with me.

Maggie What trick?

Jack Trying to divert attention from the biscuit you so greedily procured for yourself. That gorgeous, crumbly biscuit. I hope it wasn't ... Was it the *last* biscuit?

Maggie I've no idea — I think it must have been ... Do you want to share it?

Jack Of course I don't! You just enjoy it ... Every last delicious crunch of it.

Jack looks forlorn. Maggie gives in

Maggie Oh take the bloody thing. I can't stand to see children suffer.

Jack (*delighted to do so*) Thank you very much.

Jack takes Maggie's biscuit and sits himself into an armchair. He dunks the biscuit in his tea and takes a bite. It is delicious

Oh! You don't know what you're missing.

Geraldine enters from the kitchen

Geraldine Oh — so he's finally emerged, has he. Just a second — where did you find that biscuit?

Maggie I gave it to him.

Geraldine You did what!?

Maggie You should have seen his face. I'd have given him my first born child if he'd asked.

Geraldine You'll never learn. (*She tidies the cups on the table*) How's the tea?

Maggie Fine, thank you. (*To Jack*) Would have been nicer with a biscuit.

Jack takes another bite and nods in agreement

Jack What are you doing here anyway?

Maggie Have you forgotten? Dear me, you are getting old.

Jack I have other things on my mind. My life is very complicated. Just this morning, I had to pick out my own dressing gown.

Maggie Yes, you must be exhausted.

Jack So?

Maggie We have to re-sign the contracts for the Café de Paris. The originals were full of errors. So our esteemed agent dropped them off last night in a mad panic.

Jack We have to do something about him, he's utterly hopeless. Why don't we just get a *new* agent?

Maggie What's the point? It's like changing deckchairs on the *Titanic*. We're all going down in the end.

Jack Let's have them then.

Maggie They're in my coat. The big expensive new fur hanging by the door.

Jack looks at the coat

Jack I dread to think how many poor woodland creatures died in order to keep you snug. (*He fetches the contracts from the pocket of the coat*)

Maggie I've initialled everything, so you just need to sign on the final page. And try not to put "With love and best wishes" like you did last time.

Geraldine Do you want your glasses?

Jack I do not need glasses.

Geraldine (*to Maggie*) He needs his glasses. (*She goes to the piano to fetch them*)

Jack They're just for reading ... and for things that are far away. It's only when things are close up or in the distance that I have a problem. If everything in the world was twelve feet away, I'd have perfect eyesight.

Maggie So — if it's both reading *and* far distance — does that make you short-sighted or long-sighted?

Jack I don't know, I couldn't read the prescription.

Geraldine gives Jack his glasses. She takes the tea and biscuit from him as Maggie passes him a pen. Geraldine eats the rest of the biscuit as Jack signs the contract

"Thinking of you ... Jack Nightingale."

He gives the contract back to Maggie, who then also signs it. Jack reclaims his tea from Geraldine. He searches in vain for the biscuit

Where's my damn —— ? That's coming out of your wages.

Geraldine Ha! It's hardly worth signing the cheque as it is.

Jack sits in the armchair. Maggie gives the signed contracts to Geraldine

Maggie Pop those back in my coat pocket, would you.
Geraldine Of course. (*She returns the contracts to Maggie's coat pocket*)
Maggie (*to Jack*) Did you know I was invited to dinner last night?
Jack I didn't. Who would be so foolish?
Maggie The manager of the Café de Paris. Roger.
Jack Roger? I thought he was —— ?
Maggie No — you're thinking of Robert, the chef. Robert is. Or at
least he *was* for a time there. I think he likes to change the menu
every so often. But Roger is not — apparently. Well, of course, he still
might be. I've no evidence to the contrary. Not yet. We've only had
dinner. And if he wants me for dessert, it'll cost him more than a bit of
chicken pie and a shandy.
Jack You have such very high standards.
Maggie Then this morning, he sent me flowers.
Jack Did he now? Roses?
Maggie No — *lilies*. Perhaps he thinks I just died.
Jack Any flowers are a good sign.
Maggie Not necessarily.

Geraldine has returned

(*To Geraldine*) If you were an eligible bachelor taking me on a date,
Geraldine, what would you bring me? Roses or lilies?
Geraldine Diamonds.
Maggie Oh that's a good answer! You are clever. (*To Jack*) Well, that's
settled it. Geraldine will be selecting all my men from here on. But
then again, if there is just one decent man left out there, I suppose
she'll marry him herself. (*To Geraldine*) Would you consider a trip
down the aisle any time soon?
Geraldine I still feel too young for all that.
Maggie Yes, me too.

Geraldine laughs. Then she realizes it wasn't intended as a joke

Geraldine Sorry I thought you were being humorous. (*Seeking an
escape*) I'll make some more tea.

Geraldine exits into the kitchen

Maggie (*to Jack*) How much would it cost to have her killed?

Jack You can't kill her, she's the only one who knows where the kitchen is. We'd all starve. So forget it — there's nobody else to poach my eggs. And besides you shouldn't be planning murder, you should be planning another romantic tryst with you-know-who.

Maggie Who?

Jack With —— My God, you've forgotten the poor bugger already!

Maggie Oh, him.

Jack He has a name!

Maggie I *know* he does! ... Robert.

Jack Roger!

Maggie That's what I meant! Roger. Dear Roger ... Dear Roger that brought (*pulling a face*) *lilies* ...!

Jack Oh, well consign him to the dustbin, then. Unfortunate sod. You'll break his heart before he even realizes he has one.

Maggie Darling, I don't think that makes sense.

Jack It's very early. I've only had half a biscuit.

Maggie So do you really think I should have another romantic dinner with him?

Jack Why not?

Maggie I suppose he is *older* than me, which is a distinct bonus. He won't notice the cracks so much. They're not so bad now — but in ten years, I'll need scaffolding.

Jack You're always far too obsessed about your looks. Sometimes I think you quite forget how beautiful you are.

Maggie Well, you know I forget all kinds of things these days. My head's turning to marmalade ... Am I?

Jack Turning to marmalade? I've no idea.

Maggie I mean — am I beautiful you damn nitwit?!

Jack Well not so much now!

She waits

Yes, beautiful. Divine in every way.

Maggie Oh, Jack. What an unexpected compliment. (*She stands*) So now I've had my morning tea and flattery, I must be off. Remember we have a lunch meeting on Thursday.

Jack Who with?

Maggie A journalist.

Jack Will I have to be nice?

Maggie No, no — you just be yourself.

Maggie heads towards the UC *door. As she approaches it, the doorbell rings*

Jack My god, it's like Piccadilly Circus round here.
Maggie Shall I answer it?
Jack No! It might be someone important. We don't want to frighten
them off.

Geraldine enters from the kitchen

Geraldine will get it — that's what she's paid for.
Geraldine And oh so lavishly. (*She goes to the door and opens it*)

Charlie enters

Geraldine Hello, Charlie!
Charlie Hello, Geraldine. I brought you a pot of strawberry jam. (*He
hands the pot of jam to her*)
Geraldine Oh. Why?
Charlie (*thinking for a second*) Actually, I've no idea ... It'll come
back to me. (*He takes the jar back and puts it in his pocket*) Lovely
morning. Very crisp!
Geraldine Yes — freezing.
Charlie My boy here?
Geraldine Buried in that armchair somewhere — he just got up.
Jack (*not moving*) Morning, Dad.
Maggie Hello, Charlie.

Charlie sees Maggie for the first time

Charlie Hello, Maggie! You're a sight for sore eyes.

They kiss

You smell nice.
Maggie It's a new perfume with extract of apples. I think more of us
should smell of fruit, don't you?
Charlie Absolutely! You don't just smell gorgeous, you *look* gorgeous.
Are you getting younger?
Maggie Yes, I am! How clever of you to notice. Where's Beatrice?

Charlie looks at the blank space beside him

Charlie Funny — she was here a minute ago. Must be looking at the
garden or something.
Geraldine Do you want tea? (*She heads for the teapot*)
Charlie Yes, if you like. And one of those lovely biscuits.

Jack Too late. Maggie had the last one.
Maggie (*astonished*) I'm speechless!
Charlie Are you two having a rehearsal?
Maggie No, just some contracts that needed to be urgently dealt with. Our agent is always rather chaotic.
Charlie I don't like agents. They take a slice of the pie without providing any of the ingredients. We worked for forty years without an agent. I don't need someone to order me around and tell me I'm worthless — I have a wife for that.

Geraldine hands Charlie a cup of tea

Geraldine Here you go. I presume Beatrice will want one, it's very chilly out there.
Charlie Just keep it on standby.
Maggie How is she?
Charlie Beat? Fine. You know actors — we don't get old, we just lose our parts. (*He chuckles at his own joke*)
Maggie I do wish you and Beat would do your variety act again — even for just one night. People still talk about how much they loved the two of you.
Charlie Ah well — yes, it's easy to be loved when the lights are on you. It's when the lights are off that it really counts. We've been together fifty years, me and Beatrice. Both as husband and wife and as "Charlie and Beat" on the stage. She's an old whore.
Maggie (*surprised*) Your wife?
Charlie Showbusiness.
Maggie Oh? Ah yes — sorry. (*She laughs, embarassed*)
Charlie But you do it because you love it. We all do, don't we. She's a rare mistress — tough, cruel and exhausting.
Maggie Showbusiness?
Charlie No, my wife. You really are very confused.
Jack She's turning to marmalade.
Charlie Beatrice was the star, you know. Oh, I was good. But all the eyes were on her. She sparkled. You can't learn that. They can't teach someone how to sparkle ... So you never saw us?
Maggie Well, I'm sure I must have done once — when I was very young and not really paying attention. I was often at the Empire. I used to hang around with my uncle. He was a manager of sorts — used to look after Barrie Brady, the Dancing Accordionist.
Charlie Oh yes — I remember him. He was terrible. Always used to play "the haircuts".
Maggie That's right.

Geraldine Haircuts?

Charlie Final act on the bill. You perform while the audience is leaving — so all you can see is their haircuts. They'd put Barrie on at the very end of the show in order to clear the building as quickly as possible. Only a large fire could empty a theatre faster than Barrie Brady ... He died young, you know. God must have seen his act ... (*Crossing to Jack*) Jack, however, never plays to an empty seat. How's it been going, son? What have you been up to?

Jack Since dinner yesterday? Not a great deal.

Charlie They served us up a roast. Potatoes, gravy, parsnips, Yorkshire pudding. It was a feast. And we brought dessert.

Jack Yes and what lovely bananas they were. So, Dad, to what do we owe the pleasure of this particular surprise visit so early after sunrise?

Charlie I just wanted to see my boy.

Jack No, but really.

Charlie Well — I do have to ask you something, Jack. At some point — you know, when it's convenient. Could me and your mum see if we might ... find a gap in your diary to come and stay here for a few days? We just need a change of air occasionally and your mum hates being stuck in the house with me all day ... Is that something we could talk about? A little holiday for us — here at your place?

Jack I doubt that's a good idea. We argue endlessly as it is.

Charlie That's because we don't see enough of each other. So we have to save it all up. If I was here non-stop for a day or two, we'd run out of things to shout about.

Jack That's an interesting theory.

Charlie Look — it's just a casual request. I don't know (*to Maggie*) — you'd think I was asking for the world. (*Back to Jack*) It was just a thought — if the moment came when it was convenient — I only wondered if we could have a few days here, that's all.

Jack Well, I suppose ... Yes, all right.

Charlie Oh. Well, that's — that's really good of you. (*Shouting into the garden*) He said "Yes"!

Beatrice, his wife, enters, wheeling in a huge trunk on a porter's trolley

... I'll get the cases. (*To Geraldine*) Give us a hand, would you?

Charlie exits with Geraldine

Jack I thought you said if "convenient"? — Maggie — help!!

Maggie Well what do you expect me to do? I'm not family. Help your mother with that trunk or whatever it is.

Jack It's their old music hall trunk. They can store the whole bloody world in that thing.
Beatrice Morning, darling. This is very generous of you.
Jack It's not generous at all — turn around!
Beatrice Don't be silly.
Jack I mean it! You can't be here.
Beatrice Stop it now, we're *already* here. And the packing took hours. Just take a breath — breathe, darling. It'll all seem perfectly normal in the morning.

Charlie and Geraldine enter carrying two large suitcases each

Jack Just answer me this — How long are you staying *exactly*?
Charlie Just a few days ... a week — or two ... We'll be out by Christmas.
Jack It's January the seventh!
Charlie We can talk about it later. I don't want to discuss it in front of your mother — she has a weak heart.
Beatrice Only because I live with *you*.

Charlie heads to the door leading to the bedrooms, Geraldine following

Jack Just make sure those cases don't bump into the ——

At this moment, the cases Charlie is carrying slam into the door frame. Jack despairs

Charlie and Geraldine exit

Beatrice (*referring to the trunk*) This is not going to fit through the door — we'll have to park it somewhere.
Jack How about at *your* place?
Beatrice Oh, don't fret, Jack — I'm sure we'll head back there eventually.
Jack "Eventually"?

Jack manouevres the trunk to the side of the stage and offloads it from the trolley. Maggie examines it with interest

Beatrice It's just a few days — let's see what happens. I need a change of scene — desperately! We were always on the road, travelling, always on the move. Your father and I were like gypsies. And I wanted to spend every minute with him. But now we're stuck at home like a couple of concrete posts and I want to kill him. No, I mean for real — I think I could manage it with my bare hands.

Jack But we'll talk about it — yes? We *have* to talk about it.

Beatrice And we will, darling. Of course we will. We don't want to be a nuisance.

Maggie I love your trunk.

Beatrice Oh — thank you, Maggie. Isn't it wonderful? We haven't used it for travelling for years. But it's so full of useful bits and pieces, it had to come with us.

Maggie opens the door of the trunk and blows out the dust inside it. She is engulfed in a huge cloud of debris

Yes, I've been meaning to give it a good clean out.

Maggie There's dust in there that's older than I am.

Beatrice Geraldine can find us a damp cloth — give it a good rub down.

Charlie enters, now empty-handed

Where's Geraldine?

Charlie In our room.

Jack The guest room — it's called the *guest* room.

Beatrice heads for the bedrooms

Maggie Well, Jack — I really ought to be going.

Jack (*referring drily to his parents*) You're not staying till the end of the show?

Maggie No — I think I'll catch a matinee later on. See you Thursday for lunch.

Jack But I might be busy moving my parents out.

Maggie Oh, Jack — come on. You only get one set of parents in this life.

Jack (*looking at his father*) And thank God for that!

Charlie He says such funny things — sometimes I almost believe he means it.

Maggie It was nice to see you.

Charlie No, no — don't go, Maggie. We just got here. We need to catch up. Jack — tell her to stay.

Jack Actually, I rather wish you *would* stay. It would be so good to have a witness to all this. Otherwise, no one will believe it ... Have you had breakfast?

Maggie No, not even a biscuit.

Charlie Great. We'll eat together the best meal of the day. You learn to love your breakfast when you're in showbusiness. It's the only meal you don't eat nervous.

*Geraldine and Beatrice enter, each carrying a damp cloth. They head
straight for the trunk where they will proceed to wipe it down*

We'll have some eggs. Have we got eggs?

Jack Geraldine — have we got eggs? Maggie's refusing to leave before
she gets eggs.

Geraldine So that's *four* for breakfast?

Jack Yes, I suppose it is.

Geraldine I think we can cope with that.

Jack I can help. So long as we have supplies. I'll do French omelettes.

Beatrice I didn't know he could cook.

Geraldine He can't, but that's never stopped him.

Jack We'll have a nice leisurely breakfast and sort out this "situation".

Charlie It's not a situation. You make it sound negative. Some people
dream of having their parents in the same house with them.

Jack What people?

Charlie Billy Blade moved his parents in to live with him.

Jack Who the hell is ——

Charlie Billy Blade — worked on the music hall circuit — "the man
who juggles pickaxes". He moved his parents in and they never moved
out. Well, they had no choice after that show when he chopped his
hands off.

Jack And this is the best example you can come up with?

Charlie It was very short notice.

Jack Well, while I've still got ten fingers, the situation remains the
same. It just won't —— Don't you realize, I need calm, solitude.

Charlie Overrated.

Jack But I need —— Maggie, help me out here.

Maggie Don't look at me. I'm just here for the eggs.

Jack All right — two words — independence and privacy.

Charlie That's three words.

Jack Dad ——

Charlie Why do you need privacy? You never get up to anything. I still
don't see any sexy women hanging around.

Maggie And us three women thank you for that. Now excuse us while
we kill ourselves.

Charlie You two don't count — you're both virtually family. Think of
it as charity.

Jack Can't I just make a donation?

Charlie Besides — you'll hardly notice we're here.

Jack Oh come on! I've never met anyone in my life more "centre stage"
than you are.

Charlie Well at least we'll keep you amused and entertained. This place
needs a good injection of mindless stupidity. Doesn't it, Geraldine?

Geraldine Oh I don't know about that.

Geraldine turns downstage. She is wearing a pair of comedy spectacles with giant eyeballs, one of which is hanging down to her chin on a coil. There is no reaction from the others, but Geraldine laughs for her own benefit

Charlie That's the first time they've ever got a laugh.
Geraldine There are all kinds of things in here.

Charlie crosses over to the trunk

Charlie Our whole career's in there.

Geraldine brings out two British flags and waves them

Those are for the encore. When the show was going really well. (*He now brings out a bottle of whisky*) And that's for when the show's going really badly.
Geraldine Oh, it's fabulous. Like finding buried treasure. And all this make-up!
Charlie Well, you needed it. The lights were very bright in those days. You had to redden your cheeks, line your eyes. Dot the eyes too — at each end. Makes them look bigger. (*He reaches into the trunk and puts on a particularly stupid hat*) Hey, Jack — remember this hat?
Jack Of course I do. You wore it for Aunty Ella's funeral.
Charlie (*to Geraldine*) He knows our whole wardrobe. He spent his entire childhood backstage and in dressing-rooms. Seeing the make-up go on and off. The hats, the clothes. Then we'd be on stage for ten minutes — once an hour, every hour. Sometimes eight shows a day. And he'd sit in the room on his own practising the piano all the time until we came back. That's how he got so good. If we hadn't completely ignored him, he wouldn't have been the man he is today.
Geraldine What else can I try on?
Charlie How about this? (*He quickly fixes a false moustache on Geraldine*) My God it's frightening — you look just like ... Actually you don't look like anybody, it's just frightening. Do you play anything? (*He produces a small flute*)
Geraldine No, nothing.
Charlie So what *can* you do? What's your talent?
Geraldine Nothing at all. Can't play, can't sing, can't dance. That's why I've spent my life running houses for people like Jack. At least that way I can work every day with people who *can*, so that I can forget about the fact that I *can't*. On my own, I'm an artistic void.

Charlie Well, you know, God likes to spread things around — some get talent and some get intelligence ... Not sure what you got ...
Geraldine Oh thank you very much!
Charlie I'm joking. You know we love you.
Geraldine Before I've served up breakfast, everybody loves me.

The doorbell rings

Excuse me while I get that.
Jack If it's anyone else with a suitcase, tell them we're already fully booked.
Geraldine It's probably the post.

Geraldine answers the door, still wearing the comedy spectacles and moustache. Although unseen by the audience, the visitor is the postman

Morning!

Geraldine is given a handful of letters including a pink envelope, then closes the door

The postman didn't react to my face at all! Didn't even blink.
Maggie Well, once you've seen a thousand women at sunrise without make-up, nothing horrifies you.
Geraldine (*checking through the mail*) This is all for the office. Although there is one fan letter for Jack by the looks of it. (*She smells the solitary pink envelope*) Oh yes. Definitely an admirer.
Charlie What is it — perfume?
Geraldine No, *Dettol* — his fans are very old.

She gives the letter to Jack. He opens it

And one here for you, Charlie.
Charlie Oh, great. (*He takes it*)

Jack stops in his tracks

Jack How can there be?
Charlie I told the postman to bring our mail here.
Jack Isn't that a bit presumptuous?
Charlie Not at all — I knew you weren't going to throw your own parents out on the street.
Jack You have your own house!

Charlie We need company, Jack. Nobody visits anymore. (*To Maggie, sadly*) All our friends are dead.

Maggie Oh, I'm sorry.

Jack No, they're not! Don't listen to him. Last birthday, you couldn't move for all the "turns" that turned up. It was an octogenarian invasion. You know theatre people — they hear there's a free meal on offer and they can't get there fast enough.

Charlie It wasn't just that — Singalong Sally baked one of her famous birthday cakes.

Maggie Who on earth —— ?

Beatrice Singalong Sally. Used to get the crowd yelling out the old songs while she balanced a barrel of beer on her head.

Charlie She was a legend — both on stage and in the bedroom. Especially the bedroom. They said she knew every trick in the book.

Jack Dad!

Charlie What? It's only sex. We all do it. When there's a full moon, even me and your mum.

Jack I think I need to lie down.

Charlie I'm teasing you. We don't do it anymore. Everything dried up years ago.

Jack And still I need to lie down.

Charlie Never mind that. How about a nice glass of red wine?

Jack It's ten in the morning!

Charlie All right — white wine.

Geraldine Tell you what — why don't I chill a bottle for later in the day?

Jack Yes, Dad, let's not start on the alcohol till eleven a.m. — give your liver a holiday. (*To Beatrice*) I don't know how you put up with him.

Beatrice I never said that I did.

Maggie How many years has it been?

Beatrice Since what?

Maggie Your marriage.

Beatrice Oh, I try not to think about it. Raises my blood pressure.

Maggie Was it love at first sight?

Beatrice No — at first sight, I couldn't stand him.

Charlie Oh charming!

Beatrice Well, you weren't even romantic — not even on our first date.

Charlie I bought you chocolates.

Beatrice You *ate* the chocolates!

Charlie The bus was late! I had nothing else to do.

Beatrice (*to Maggie*) You see my point? Anyway — somehow we still ended up together. For better or worse ... mostly worse, now I think of it.

Maggie I'd love to be married.

Beatrice I'm sure you'd make a lovely bride. Not sure that *I* was. Charlie didn't give *me* much time to think about it. It was a spur of the moment thing. Very impulsive — suddenly there we were, signing the register in the town hall. I thought we were just going out for a bag of chips. But if you want marriage — then you *will* be married. That's what I believe. It's only a matter of time. That goes for Jack too.

Jack I doubt that very much.

Beatrice Cupid is waiting out there right now to fire an arrow at your heart.

Jack It won't penetrate. He'll need a machine gun. And besides — how am I ever going to even attempt romance with my parents living here? That kicks all hopes of passion right off the field.

Beatrice Jack — you know if at any time you really want us to leave — I mean, joking aside, if you *really* want us to leave — all you have to say is this — "Mum, Dad, I love you, but I need time to myself and so you have to move back to your own house right now." And we will go.

Jack Really?

Beatrice Really.

Jack Mum, Dad, I love you, but I need time to myself and ——

Beatrice interrupts, breaking from him and approaching Geraldine

Beatrice Not now, darling, I'm talking to Geraldine.

Geraldine Yes?

Beatrice Is there any *cake*?

Geraldine Cake? We have a fresh Victoria sponge.

Beatrice Oh, yes, please.

Geraldine Charlie?

Charlie Does it come with a glass of sherry?

Jack No, it doesn't, funnily enough. (*To Geraldine*) Just put the entire thing on the piano. You know they eat like tigers.

Geraldine exits into the kitchen

Charlie You're always hungry if you work on the stage.

Maggie But doesn't the habit change when you retire?

Charlie You see, I don't think of myself as having retired. I see this as an intermission. An incredibly long intermission.

Beatrice He'd have me back on the road singing and dancing for my supper if he had his way. Playing every collapsing theatre and downmarket flea pit in the country. That's the problem with actors like Charlie — they never stop acting!

Charlie (*theatrically*) How *dare* you ..!

Jack You won't change him now.

Beatrice Oh I know that! The only way to stop Charlie performing would be to whack him across the head with a large shovel.

Jack Really? (*Calling out*) Geraldine!

Beatrice (*to Charlie*) Now make yourself useful and start the unpacking.

Charlie Unpack!? I don't do unpacking! What a waste of my talent. Besides — I don't know where to put anything.

Beatrice Socks in the sock drawer, knickers in the knicker drawer and after that just let your imagination run riot!

Charlie I refuse! I once played King Lear!

Beatrice Yes — you *once* played King Lear. The show closed the next morning.

Charlie (*as King Lear*) "Blow winds! Crack your cheeks!"

Geraldine enters and looks to Jack to see what he wants

Geraldine Did you need something?

Jack Yes — find me a large *shovel*, would you?

Geraldine Shovel?

Maggie He's joking.

Jack Don't be so certain.

Charlie I'd like to give my Lear again.

Beatrice It won't be any better. It'll now just come with creaking bones and added flatulence.

Charlie I never broke wind during a performance.

Beatrice (*to the others*) Actually, that's true — he always saved it for when we returned to the dressing-room. I'm a very lucky woman. Now, please Charlie — the unpacking.

Charlie On my own!?

Maggie Jack will help you.

Jack No I won't! I don't do unpacking!

Maggie No wonder they don't get on — like peas in a pod. Come on, I'll give you a hand.

Maggie heads for the door. Jack and Charlie don't move

... Now!!

Charlie and Jack follow like naughty schoolchildren. They exit

Beatrice and Geraldine are now alone

Beatrice At last! A bit of peace and quiet. (*She sits down*)

Geraldine Can I get you something to drink?

Beatrice No — come and sit down.

Geraldine I have to get on with breakfast.
Beatrice No — come on — it's not often I get someone different to talk to.
Geraldine All right — if you insist.
Beatrice I do.

Geraldine sits with her

That was one of the nice things about touring all the time — there were always lots of people milling around, stage hands, ushers. Some of the acts also had apprentices — watching the show every day with the idea that they would take over when all us old buggers couldn't hack it anymore. Very nice young chaps some of them. Though we knew they were really wasting their time. Variety was dying faster than we all were. And when it disappeared, we all vanished along with it. I miss all those nice young chaps.
Geraldine So there, you see, you do miss some things about it.
Beatrice Well, I mean, I've yet to meet a woman who tires of being around enthusiastic young men. In the days before I married, I spent every minute backstage, flirting with the boys. But we were always on tour and off the following week, so there was never a chance to do anything more about it. I had the desire, but not the time. And now of course ...
Geraldine You've got the time but not the desire.
Beatrice Precisely.
Geraldine One day, you must show me all your souvenirs. Of the act, I mean. The tours you went on, the theatres you played, the posters and costumes — I bet it's fascinating.
Beatrice I expect it's all in a box hidden away somewhere.
Geraldine Then you should find it.
Beatrice Why?
Geraldine For me. For Jack. Well, not just us, actually — for future generations. Maybe one day they'll build a museum with all of you music hall performers in it.
Beatrice Yes, they could have us all stuffed.
Geraldine Otherwise it just disappears, like you say.
Beatrice Well, that's life, isn't it? That's how it's meant to be. We're here and then one day everything just goes. All of it. And before that, of course, you have the joys of old age to conjure with. We always used to get a lovely round of applause as we walked onstage. Now we should get a round of applause for the fact we can walk at all. When it's over, it's over. If anyone was that interested to see us, they should have bought a ticket.
Geraldine Yes, but what about in a hundred years' time?

Beatrice No one will care. They'll all be living on the moon.
Geraldine People will always remember you and Charlie.
Beatrice Even *this week*, people don't remember me and Charlie.
That's showbusiness.
Geraldine I think that you should write it all down. Your whole life.
Now you're here — you've plenty of time to do that.
Beatrice An autobiography? No, I don't think so.
Geraldine People would be fascinated.
Beatrice Nonsense. People only read autobiographies for the scandal.
The books are not a success unless you've been to bed with eighty-two
people in the first three chapters.

Geraldine looks at her

And no, Geraldine — I haven't done that. I would never have got any
knitting done.
Geraldine I think that's a shame.
Beatrice Oh, so do I!

Geraldine laughs

Geraldine The book, I mean. Things shouldn't just vanish.
Beatrice Well, of course, we did let them *film* the act.
Geraldine Well — there you are.
Beatrice We were all doing it. The money was quite good. But of
course it killed us all really. The theatres started showing little films
in amongst the live acts and soon realized that if they had you on film,
they never needed to hire the real thing again. Rather than presenting
the act, they just switched the projector on. And that was the end of
you. We should never have done it. It was vanity, of course. And it
turned round and *bit* us. But you live and learn. And when you've
lived as long as I have — oh, you've learned far too much ... And what
about you? What's your story?
Geraldine I don't have a story. I just get the breakfast.
Beatrice But you're so lovely — there must be the perfect young man
out there somewhere.
Geraldine When do *I* have the time to go courting?
Beatrice But after opening nights, this place is often full of men.
Geraldine Actors and agents!?!
Beatrice Oh yes, you do have a point.
Geraldine Anyway, I never abandon my theatrical gentlemen. I stay till
they don't need me anymore.
Beatrice Will my Jack ever marry again, do you think?

Geraldine I don't know. Only he can answer that. And now I really
   must ——
Beatrice Yes, yes — you get on with whatever you need to do. I'll
   just —— (*She looks around*) Actually, I might have a go on the piano,
   if I may?
Geraldine That would be lovely.

*They both get up. Geraldine heads for the kitchen, as Beatrice heads for
the piano*

   We love hearing the piano in this house.
Beatrice I'm a bit out of practice.
Geraldine I'm sure you'll play wonderfully.

*Beatrice sits at the piano. She begins to play a melody on it. At first she
plays moderately well, but it soon falls apart and she proceeds to play
very badly — every fifth note hilariously wrong*

   Jack and Charlie enter. They listen in horror

Jack (*to Charlie*) Why is Mother at the piano?
Charlie I have no idea.
Jack We have to find a way of stopping her from doing that.

*Beatrice ends the piano playing with an awful flourish. She then proudly
steps out from behind the piano*

Beatrice That was better than I thought. Just a little bit of extra practice
   and I'll be perfect ... My piano playing used to charm the birds out of
   the trees.
Charlie Now they *throw* themselves out of the trees ..!
Beatrice What did you think, Jack?
Jack It was ... very surprising.
Charlie Surprisingly awful!
Jack Dad! That's very inconsiderate.
Charlie I'm just telling the truth.
Jack You of all people should know that when a performer or musician
   asks you what you think — they don't actually want to know what
   you *think*. They just want you to say they were marvellous. It's not
   a question, it's the opening of a door to welcome in a hurricane of
   compliments. You're expected to oblige.
Charlie In my day — we just told the truth.
Jack Well, times have changed. In *modern* showbusiness, we hide our true
   feelings, lie and speak with complete dishonesty. It's called progress.

Charlie You're too soft — that's your problem. Too sensitive.

Jack Fine. Good. I'll take that as a compliment.

Charlie You can't — it wasn't meant as a compliment.

Beatrice Oh God, I wish I'd never asked.

Jack (*to Charlie*) Your generation is too hard — too cold. No wonder all your sons and daughters got messed up.

Charlie Messed up? Look at you in your big house with your evenings at the Café de Paris and your summer cruises. If that's messed up — I'll take a dozen. And to think I taught you everything you know.

Jack Oh come off it — you were never there. You were always out of town doing your stupid act.

Charlie Stupid!? How dare you. I think what you do is more stupid. Sitting at a piano singing Cole Porter — all elegant and witty with champagne up your arse.

Jack People like it.

Charlie People like to paint. Doesn't mean they want to spend the whole evening watching it dry.

Jack You've become a cantankerous old bugger in your old age. No — not just now — always. Even when I was a kid, you were bloody-minded and appallingly difficult.

Charlie How do you know? I was never there.

Jack Believe me — you made a full impression during your brief appearances.

Charlie I may not have been the ideal father — but we loved you. We loved you and never said a bad word about you — you ungrateful bastard.

Jack Why the hell did you come here? Why!? Simply to drive me up the wall?

Charlie Don't look at me — it was your mother's idea.

Jack looks questioningly at his mother

She just made me do all the dirty work. I wanted to go to a beach hut in Walton-on-the-Naze.

Jack It's never too late to get what you want. I hear Walton-on-the-Naze is lovely at this time of year — wherever the hell it is. I'll pay for the hut myself. Let me book it right away. (*He picks up the telephone*)

Beatrice Stop it now.

Jack He always does this. He finds my weak point and shoves a tent pole into it.

Beatrice Put the phone down — we are staying here.

Jack No, Mum — no! I mean it. Visiting is one thing, but ——

Beatrice Just a few days — all right? Just a few days. It's important.

Jack Why? I don't ——
Beatrice A few more days and then we go.
Jack What is going on? There's something going on — I know there is.
Beatrice Jack ——
Jack What is it? Tell me.
Beatrice Nothing. I promise you. We just needed a little break, that's all. And I'm not going to bloody Walton on the whatever it is. Why do you always have to read conspiracy into everything? I just thought it would be nice to have a break and spend a bit of time with our boy. ... It's just flustered you, that's all. You're overreacting. But it's all right — we'll be gone by the weekend.
Jack *This* weekend?
Beatrice I don't know *which* weekend — you're so preoccupied with details. But can we please just call a truce and not discuss it any more for the moment.

Jack slumps into his armchair

Now did you at least get some of the unpacking done?
Charlie No — we were too busy arguing.
Beatrice I despair of both of you!

Geraldine and Maggie enter carrying trays of breakfast foods. They put the trays on top of the piano

All grab a plate and some food, which they consume during the following dialogue. Charlie grabs a cup of coffee

Geraldine There's coffee or tea. Charlie — do you want a drop of liqueur in your coffee? (*She fetches the liqueur decanter*)
Charlie Thank you, Geraldine. I like a nice drop of liqueur.
Jack You like a nice drop of everything.
Maggie Still arguing, are they?
Beatrice Afraid so.
Charlie Heavy drinking is how I was brought up. Everyone drinks in showbusiness. It's part of the religion. All talented people drink too much.
Jack *I* don't drink too much.
Charlie I rest my case.

Geraldine holds the decanter above Charlie's cup, waiting to pour it

Geraldine Say when.

Charlie *Now* would be fine.

Geraldine pours the liqueur into Charlie's cup

Maggie I think I might have a drop of that. Are you having one too, Geraldine?

Geraldine Don't worry about me. I always sneak one when none of you are looking.

Maggie I bet you get up to all sorts of things when we're not looking ..

Geraldine Oh, if only that were true ...

Charlie I think it's a sign of the times.

Jack What is?

Charlie That you can't speak your mind.

Jack Oh God ...

Charlie When we played the circuit, the theatre managers would tell us exactly what was on their mind. Notes, criticism, change this in the act, change that. You listened, you accepted it, you did what you were told. Remember the Royal?

Beatrice Johnny Ruby.

Charlie When Johnny Ruby ran the place, he wanted all acts to be ten minutes. Not a second more. So we had to cut it down — cut an act we'd been doing for twenty years. But he was the law. He wanted his variety shows to run like buses. So if you get some magician or singer up there who's a stinker, the audience don't mind 'cos —

Beatrice There'll be another one along in ten minutes.

Charlie But now it seems they're all so sensitive, you can't say anything to them. (*He sips his coffee*) Can you put more alcohol in this Geraldine? The first lot's evaporated.

Geraldine does so to Jack's disapproval

Jack No more than an extra dribble.

Charlie Don't know why you never drank more, Jack.

Jack Nor do I. I've had plenty of reasons to.

Geraldine I think he does well enough. He drinks plenty of champagne during the shows. It's all devastatingly sophisticated.

Beatrice Now where does he get all that sophistication from? It's not from me, is it, Jack? And it's *certainly* not from your father.

Maggie If you're going to sing witty charming songs at the piano, people demand that you yourself are witty and charming. Simple as that. We're complete fakes.

Geraldine But you both fake it beautifully. People assume Jack comes from some terribly wealthy, elegant family.

Beatrice (*to Jack*) And when they ask, do you tell them the truth?

Jack Of course not. I tell them you're a barrister and a duchess.

Charlie Why!? There's nothing shameful about living your life on stage.

Beatrice No, but it's hardly elegant!

Charlie Theatrical performers *are* elegant! Elegant right up to their armpits! You never realized your luck. I don't understand why you don't miss it. Why it doesn't drive you mad that we're not on stage anymore.

Beatrice I do miss it — very occasionally. I'm just not convinced it was the perfect life. Far from it.

Charlie I've had it with all this. I'm going back to bed!

Beatrice *Before* breakfast?!

Charlie storms into the bedroom, grabbing a handful of sandwiches as he goes

Geraldine I'll, erm — I'll bring him some napkins.

Geraldine grabs a few napkins and follows Charlie off

Maggie I don't mean to interfere, but your family really must find a better way of communicating — you know, not shouting at each other, for example.

Jack It won't change now. Not after all these years. When they dropped in for dinner, I could cope. Button my lip. But here all the time?

Beatrice You just need to relax more — calm yourself down. That's what I *try* and do. Maggie is absolutely right. We need to not get agitated. We have to seek calm and serenity.

Jack If there's any calm and serenity on offer, I'll take a gallon, please.

Beatrice Tell you what — I'll play something for you on the piano. That always used to calm you down when you were a baby.

Jack That was a *long* time ago.

Beatrice Oh, just do as you're told. The doctor says you shouldn't disagree with me — it's bad for my kidney.

Jack But is this something you've practised? You know how you play when you don't practise.

Beatrice Yes, yes. This one's my speciality. (*She sits at the piano*) So — shut your eyes and ... *Relax* ...

Jack shuts his eyes, taking deep breaths. Beatrice begins to play a popular lullaby on the piano. She plays a little better than before, and the opening bars are perfect. But she then starts to hit the occasional misplaced note — some of them agonizingly wrong. Jack winces at each error. She perseveres until Jack cannot stand any more. He gets out of the chair and charges to the piano

Jack Stop! Stop!!
Beatrice The piano needs tuning.
Jack No, Mother, your *fingers* need tuning.
Beatrice I was trying to help you relax.
Jack I was more relaxed during D-Day! Swap over.
Beatrice But ——
Jack Armchair! And not another word.

Beatrice takes her place in the armchair. Jack sits at the piano

Maggie Somebody should write a play about this family.
Jack Somebody did, but the audience didn't believe it!

Maggie laughs and then takes a seat on the sofa

Beatrice Jack — let me have another go.
Maggie No, no — leave him to it. This is a good idea. This will calm him. I've even on occasion seen Jack drop off to sleep at the piano.
Beatrice Not during a show, I hope?
Jack Just the once. And oddly — nobody seemed to notice.
Maggie That's because they were all looking at *me*, darling. Now are you going to play the bloody lullaby or do we need the understudy?
Jack I'm just warming up my hands.
Beatrice That's *his* way of saying he can't remember the tune.
Jack Could you be quiet, please ... Thank you.

Jack begins to play the lullaby at the piano. He does so beautifully. If the actor playing the role can carry a tune, he might also hum or sing a few lyrics. Within a few bars, we notice that both Maggie and Beatrice are nodding off. By the time Jack finishes playing, they are both asleep. Beatrice is snoring. Jack finishes playing the tune

On the final note, the Lights fade to black-out

During the scene change, music of the 1950s period is heard — Garland, Astaire, Coward, Sinatra, etc.

SCENE 2

The same. A day later. The middle of the night

The living-room is empty. Lit only by moonlight through the curtains and a solitary corner lamp. After a moment, the door leading to the bedrooms slowly and silently opens. A suitcase comes into view and is placed just inside the door. The door closes again. A few seconds and it opens once more. Beatrice emerges, fully dressed including hat and coat. She is carrying a second suitcase. She checks the room is empty, then also picks up the first case and creeps silently towards the front door. When halfway there, the bedroom hall light switches on. Beatrice panics — not wanting to be seen — and scurries to hide behind the trunk with her cases. Jack enters, in his pyjamas, and turns on a lamp. He surveys the room. He picks up a newspaper and sits down to read it. He realizes he can't make out any of the words

Jack Oh, bloody hell.

He looks around for his glasses and checks near to the drinks cabinet. The glasses not in sight, he picks up the brandy decanter and pours himself a drink. He wanders over to the trunk to occupy himself. He opens it up and looks inside. Beatrice's head pops up from behind it

Beatrice Jack.

Jack lets out an almighty scream

(*In hushed tones*) Don't scream! — what are you screaming for? Keep your voice down.
Jack You frightened the life out of me. What are you doing there?
Beatrice Nothing.
Jack Nothing?
Beatrice I like it here. I was — I couldn't sleep, I was going to go for a walk.
Jack At four a.m?
Beatrice In the moonlight. Lots of people like to do that.
Jack Yes — cat burglars and vampires. Have you gone mad?
Beatrice Yes — yes, I think I have.
Jack I could have had a heart attack.
Beatrice Well, you didn't. Go back to bed.

Geraldine enters hurriedly through the kitchen door, wearing her nightie and a scruffy old jumper. She is holding a rolling pin and a large whisk

Geraldine I'm here!

Jack looks at her

Jack Yes you are — it's all right. It was just Mother.
Geraldine You screamed!
Jack She surprised me. It's all right.
Geraldine Oh God — I thought there was a burglar.
Beatrice No — sorry.

Geraldine turns the room lights on

Jack Just as a point of interest — if it *had* been a burglar, what were you going to do? *Whisk* him to death?
Geraldine Yes — or bake him a pie. (*Explaining*) They were the nearest things. (*She puts the items down on the nearest table*) What are you doing here at this time of night?
Jack I'll ask the questions, if you don't mind. (*To Beatrice*) What are you doing here at this time of night?

Beatrice moves out from behind the trunk and heads for the armchair

Beatrice I told you. I wanted a walk. I couldn't sleep. I've a lot on my mind.
Jack Like what?
Beatrice Nothing. Just go back to sleep.
Jack I wasn't asleep. That's why I was here. I kept having nightmares. You know — anxiety dreams, going on stage and realizing I was naked, that kind of thing. It's perfectly normal.
Geraldine Is it? Sounds a bit weird.
Jack Not as weird as your night clothes.
Geraldine (*realizing*) Oh yes — sorry. I'll find a dressing gown.
Jack No — go back to bed.
Geraldine I won't be able to get back to sleep. Once I'm up, I'm up. I might as well bake that pie. (*Noticing Beatrice*) Why are you *really* in a coat?
Beatrice Does nobody *ever* go out for a walk at night here?
Geraldine Actually — no.
Beatrice Well, amongst *my* generation it's perfectly normal. When you have to get up three times a night to have a pee, sometimes you just decide to make more of an event out of it. I wanted to see the stars. Orion's chariot or whatever it is ... Is that a brandy?
Jack (*still holding the brandy in his hand*) Yes.

Beatrice You were here drinking alone in the middle of the night? Oh Jack — that's not very promising.

Jack I was looking for my glasses.

Beatrice (*sarcastically*) Oh, well that makes perfect sense.

Geraldine Shall I grab a dressing gown then?

Beatrice No — go back to bed. Both of you. I was here to — to be alone. Can't I have some time alone?

Jack No you can't — now take your coat off.

Beatrice I want to go out for a walk.

Jack Then I'll come with you.

Beatrice Jack! For goodness' sake — for once, can't you just do as you're told?

Jack All right — all right. Geraldine — find me my glasses, please, and I'll take the newspaper to bed.

Geraldine quickly locates both the glasses and the newspaper

(*To Beatrice*) You don't go beyond the garden, do you hear me? And if anyone tries to bite your neck, you come straight back in.

Beatrice Fine.

Jack And drink this brandy before you go out. (*He gives her the brandy*) And wrap up warm.

Beatrice I thought *I* was the mother.

Jack At this moment, you don't qualify.

Suddenly, Charlie bursts into the room. He is wearing his wife's pink dressing gown and a pair of socks. He has his fists clenched ready for battle

Charlie Come on then, let's see what you're made of!

Beatrice Oh, Christ!

Jack Aren't you a bit late? I screamed two whole minutes ago.

Charlie I couldn't find my socks.

Jack If a burglar ever does turn up, I might as well just give him the keys.

Charlie So what's the — why did you —

Jack It's nothing. We're all retiring. Just turn around and go straight back to bed.

Charlie I need a pee.

Jack Then have a pee, just —— (*putting his face in his hands*) How did my life get so complicated?

Charlie crosses to the bathroom

Charlie I still don't get why you screamed? It was *you* I presume? It was pretty theatrical.

Jack You can have the whole story at breakfast. Good-night.

Charlie exits into the bathroom. Jack grabs his glasses and newspaper and exits to the bedrooms. Geraldine exits through the kitchen door

Beatrice is alone again, debating what she should now do

Beatrice I can't ... I can't ...

We hear a taxi pull up outside, the headlights shining through the window. Beatrice decides to take her chance. She drinks the brandy in one gulp, then dashes to the suitcases, picks them both up and goes to the front door. She opens it to exit with the cases

To Beatrice's surprise, as she opens the door, Maggie bursts into the room. She is carrying a bedraggled bunch of lilies and her mascara has run down her face because she has been crying

Maggie Oh thank God you're up! (*She storms into the middle of the room*) I didn't know where to go. I need a drink. (*She heads for the drinks cabinet*)

Beatrice looks at her and at the cab she arrived in. She exits out of the house without another word, closing the door behind her

Unaware of this, Maggie continues

I've had it with men. I mean it. I'm going to become a nun. Lilies — again! I mean — do people not *learn*. (*She throws the flowers dismissively to one side, then proceeds to pour herself a brandy*) I don't know what I would have done if your light hadn't been on. Turned the taxi round, I suppose. Or not — no, I'd have just woken you all up. You're my family — you know — you really are. (*She now grabs the whisky bottle and tops up the brandy with a large shot of whisky*) I'm so sorry. It's just all so desperate, you know. It never gets any easier ... I just don't know how much longer we're supposed to put ourselves through this. I mean at some point — at *some point* — you have to just bring down the bloody curtain. (*She now adds some gin to her potent cocktail*) I have tried — oh yes. Jack doesn't think I have — but I have. You know that. You've seen me try. But it just never seems to work. It can't go on like this. (*She scans the remaining bottles*) Isn't there any sherry?

We now hear and see the taxi drive off

... Oh well. (*She takes a gulp of her drink. It is vile. She coughs and splutters*) Oh God — how do people drink this stuff?

Charlie emerges from the bathroom

Maggie turns to see him

Charlie! Oh you're up too? That's a lovely —— is that your regular dressing gown?

Charlie I just had a pee.

Maggie Oh — how was it?

Charlie Uneventful. Where did you — when did you —— ?

Maggie Um?

Charlie I didn't know you were ——

Maggie No, of course, sorry — I just arrived in a taxi. Beatrice let me in. (*She gestures to Beatrice, who is no longer there*) Oh. Where did she —— ? Did she go outside? I hope she's not tipping the driver — I already tipped the driver. I told him to stay single. The best tip he'll ever get.

Geraldine now enters, wearing her dressing gown

Geraldine Maggie?

Maggie Oh, Geraldine — sorry to wake you.

Geraldine No, you didn't wake anybody. It's like Clapham Junction here tonight. Something up?

Maggie I just had the world's *worst* romantic dinner. Third date.

Geraldine Oh dear — third date. That one should end up in the bedroom.

Maggie No — no more of that. I am ceasing all bedroom activity. I'm shutting up my vagina for the winter.

Geraldine Ah — well, I'll inform the newspapers ... How can I help?

Maggie A drink would be very much appreciated. (*Referring to her cocktail*) This one's not very good.

Geraldine Sherry?

Maggie Yes — yes. Sherry. You see — you know exactly what a desperate woman wants. Why don't you come and work for me? I'll underpay you exactly the same amount.

Geraldine locates the sherry bottle from a small cabinet elsewhere in the room

Geraldine Sorry — not available. Do you want a sherry, Charlie?
Charlie No — I'll take that one. (*He points to Maggie's cocktail and crosses to take it from her*) What's in it?
Maggie Everything I could get my hands on.
Charlie My favourite recipe.

Jack enters from the bedroom, wearing his glasses

Jack I fell asleep. For the first time in my life, I went back to bed — and fell asleep again. That *never* happens. And yet a few seconds later, fate intervenes: Hello, Maggie.
Maggie Hello, Jack.
Jack Yes, I thought the voice I heard might be yours. I mean — who else? Have you been crying?

Maggie nods

Was it Robert?
Maggie (*correcting him*) Roger.
Jack Oh yes, that's right. Well, I presume now it doesn't matter *what* his name is.
Geraldine Sherry?
Jack Well, now I'm up. (*Looking at Charlie's drink*) What is that?
Charlie Maggie made it.
Jack You shouldn't encourage him. All right — sit down and tell me all about it. No — hang on. Get Mother in first. It's freezing out there.
Charlie I don't know where she is.
Jack She went into the garden.
Charlie Why?
Maggie To let me in. Then she didn't come back ... oddly.
Jack She does four a.m. walks now. It's another little eccentricity she's developed. (*He goes to the front door*)
Charlie So it was a man, was it? The reason for the ——
Maggie Yes. A bad date.
Charlie I'm sorry to hear that. Well — you know — all men are bastards.
Maggie Except for you.
Charlie No, I was including me.

Jack opens the door

Jack (*calling out*) Mum!? Come on in now — you'll catch your death.

Charlie But remember — the trials of the heart are temporary. It'll sort itself out. Never fear — your vagina will be back in business before you know it.

Geraldine brings Maggie a glass of sherry

Geraldine They should put that on a poster.
Maggie Thank you, Geraldine.
Jack Mum!?
Geraldine It's all right — I'll pop out and find her. Here's your sherry.

Jack comes back into the room and takes his sherry

Jack She promised to stay in the garden.
Geraldine Well she can't have gone far.

Geraldine grabs a scarf from the coat stand, plus keys from a nearby hook on the wall and exits out the front door, closing it behind her

Jack So — let's start at the beginning.
Maggie Oh I don't want to talk about it.
Jack You took a cab here from London at four a.m. and got us all out of bed — and now you don't want to talk about it?!
Maggie It's the age-old story. Girl wants boy. Boy wants girl. Boy is a moron.
Charlie I think they must have changed the story.

Maggie starts crying

Jack Dad — maybe Maggie would prefer if it was just the two of us?
Maggie No — I don't mind. Maybe you can give me advice, Charlie? I mean you've been married all your life, haven't you?
Charlie Yes.
Maggie Living with someone your whole life.
Charlie Yes.
Maggie In love for your whole life.
Charlie (*uncertainly*) Well ...
Maggie That's all I want. Is it too much to ask? (*To Jack*) Is it?
Jack Yes, my sweet — maybe it is.

Nothing is said for a moment. They all take a drink

It'll be all right. (*He gives her a little kiss on the cheek or forehead*)

Maggie I don't believe that any more.
Jack Oh, Maggie.

We hear another car pull up and see the headlights through the window

Your date hasn't followed you!?
Maggie Of course not. That's absurd. Don't be ridiculous. He wouldn't
... Oh God — I'll hide in the toilet.

Maggie heads into the bathroom

Charlie (*clenching his fist*) I'll sort him out.
Jack You'll do no such thing. If there's any of that to be done — *I'll* deal
with it, I'll — scratch his eyes out. On second thoughts, let's just not
let him in. He *is* quite *big*, if I remember. (*He goes to the window by
the front door and looks out through the curtains*) Ah — Geraldine's
talking to the driver. She'll sort it out. (*He shuts the curtains fully and
then goes to the bathroom door and knocks on it*) Maggie — we're
just not going to let him come in. So you might as well come out of
there. (*To Charlie*) And will you please get rid of that drink. Have a
sherry. Here — I'll swap you.

*Jack swaps his sherry for Charlie's cocktail and then deposits the
cocktail on the piano*

During this, Maggie emerges from the bathroom

Maggie On second thoughts — invite the moron in. I've got a few more
things to tell him. And I can stick those lilies up his ——
Jack There will be no sticking of lilies up anywhere. (*Realizing*) He
bought you *lilies* again?!
Maggie Yes! Three dates and not an inch of progress.

The car now drives off

Jack Ah — there — he's gone. Good job too — I fight like a twelve-
year-old girl.

The door opens and Geraldine enters, keys in hand

So — was it Maggie's fella?
Geraldine No. It was —— the taxi was here to collect Beatrice. To take
her to Dover.

Jack Take her to Dover?!
Charlie That's a bit of a trek just to go for a walk.
Geraldine I think she must have gone in the earlier taxi — Maggie's taxi — he was expecting her to have suitcases.
Jack I'm very confused.
Charlie Let me see if she's taken the cases.

Charlie heads through the door to the bedrooms

Jack Where was she going?
Geraldine On a trip I presume.
Jack A trip?
Geraldine A cruise, a ferry — I mean — that's why people go to Dover with suitcases isn't it?
Maggie Where was she going?
Jack I have no idea. It can't be. I mean — she would at least have left a note.

Charlie enters, a note in his hand, which he is reading

Dad?
Charlie She's left me, Jack. It just says — she doesn't want to be with me anymore. So she's gone to France. Beatrice has left me and gone to France.
Jack What? (*He takes the letter from Charlie and reads it*)
Charlie Now I know that's why we came here. So I wouldn't be left on my own in the house ... when she goes. That's typical of Beatrice — she thinks of everything ...

The song "La Mer" begins to play as the Lights very slowly fade to black-out

CURTAIN

ACT II

SCENE 1

The song "La Mer" plays again and the Lights slowly come up

Everything is exactly as it was at the end of Act I. The music fades out and the action continues

Maggie Jack ..?

Jack My God ... Mother really has gone ... She set the whole thing up. Moved both of you in here, so she could leave you with us while she ——

Charlie Floats off to France. Is she coming back?

Jack Of course she's coming back. (*To Maggie*) Is she coming back?

He gives Maggie the letter. Maggie reads it. Jack turns to Geraldine

Geraldine — can you find out when the next ship goes out — and where it ends up?

Geraldine I'm sure we've got a timetable in the kitchen somewhere.

Geraldine exits through the door to the kitchen

Jack (*to Charlie*) And you had no clue at all about this?

Charlie Of course not.

Jack Has it been very bad recently? Have you two been arguing all the time?

Charlie Not *all* the time. Even *I* have to sleep.

Jack I can't believe she did this. We could have at least all talked about it. And anyway — why France? You both hate the French.

Charlie Not all the French. Just the ones that come to England.

Jack Does she know anybody there?

Charlie I'd have to think about that.

Jack (*annoyed*) So think then!

Charlie Hey — don't you start with me! I'm suffering enough as it is.

Jack All right, all right — I'm sorry. I just — is there someone she might be planning to stay with? Do you know anyone French?

Charlie There were the Can-Can girls that played the circuit. We knew them quite well.

Jack And they lived where? Lyon? Bordeaux?
Charlie Colchester.
Jack Right — so *not* in France, then. You get what I'm driving at — people that *live* in France.
Charlie Give me a minute. (*He sits down to ponder*)
Maggie I think —— (*She gestures*)

Jack crosses to Maggie

(*Under her breath*) It doesn't sound temporary. The tone of the letter, it's —— There's no sense that this is a holiday. There's nothing about coming back.
Jack This is a nightmare. I don't even —— What do I do?

Geraldine returns from the kitchen

Geraldine There's one at seven a.m. — goes to Calais. Then it's two hours before the next one, so ——
Jack She's going to Calais.
Charlie Oh, we *do* know somebody in Calais.
Jack Yes?
Charlie Jean Paul Rabert. But we called him Rabbit.
Maggie Why?
Charlie Because we couldn't pronounce Rabert.
Jack Who is he?
Charlie Sang songs and danced a bit — like a gypsy. You know, all tan and earrings.
Jack And were you close? Good friends?
Charlie He got on well with Beat. She used to play cards with him backstage. And sometimes he'd show her a few of his moves.
Jack But you don't think she and Rabert could be —— ?
Maggie At it like rabbits.
Jack Maggie!
Maggie I'm just trying to move things along a bit quicker.
Charlie I don't have a clue — this is all new to me. I don't think she operates in that department much anymore.
Geraldine But isn't the issue here ——

They all look at Geraldine

— Well, I mean — It's not really about *why* she's gone — or even who she might be going to. Surely it's about stopping her going in the first place?
Jack Yes, I suppose — yes, that's right. So —— ?

Geraldine Dover. We can drive now to Dover. Talk to her.
Jack Yes — yes! Right — everybody grab what you need!

Charlie exits into the bedroom

Jack starts grabbing items from around the room. Maggie goes and grabs her coat. Geraldine watches the madness for a few seconds and then calls a halt to it

Geraldine Hang on! Hang on!

They stop

We can't *all* go. It has to be handled delicately. Remember she doesn't actually want to be stopped.
Jack Then I should just drive there on my own, do you think?
Geraldine You driving a car to the south coast? At night? I don't think so. You're the worst driver I've ever met. I'll be surprised if you made it out of the garage in one piece.
Maggie Well, *I* could go. Woman to woman, you know. We can talk about men. And what bloody sods they are.
Jack No, no — that might not be productive — I can go — give me a map and a set of rosary beads and I'll be fine.
Geraldine But it should be Charlie.
Jack She just *left* Charlie.
Geraldine Which is why it has to be him to persuade her to come home. It's no good you dragging her back and then she takes one look at him and bolts out the door again. You just need to have them talk and — well, hope for the best.
Jack No, I don't agree.
Maggie I do. Jack — I think that's the right thing.
Jack Really?
Geraldine I can drive him down there. I'll just stay in the car and let them talk.
Jack But you have to make sure she comes home.
Maggie Just let what happens — happen. Now stop yapping about it. They've got to get moving.

Charlie enters with a bag stuffed with a few items

Charlie Right — get the car ready. But I'm not having Jack drive. He's too dangerous.
Jack What is all this? I've never had an accident in my life.
Charlie No, but you've *caused* thousands.

Geraldine *I'm* driving. Do you want me to grab anything for us to eat on the way down? It might be a long night.
Charlie Yes, good idea. Just some bread and cheese, a few crisps. Maybe some fruit and — bring the jam sponge from yesterday.
Jack You're not going on a picnic!
Charlie So what — now you want me to starve!?
Jack (*to Geraldine*) Just grab whatever's handy.

Geraldine exits to the kitchen

(*To Charlie*) Maggie thinks it's best that you go on your own — just you and Geraldine. We'll stay here. OK? But —— You know, you need to think.
Charlie I know I do! ... What about?
Jack Well, some kind of strategy. What you're going to say? What you can say to bring her back.
Charlie How do I know that, you blithering idiot, when I don't know why she left in the first bloody place!
Jack Isn't it obvious!?
Charlie Yes — I see your point! (*He marches to the door and grabs his coat*)

Maggie helps him put it on

... She just got bored. That's what all this is about.
Jack Then she could have taken you with her. You could have sat by the Seine and got bored out of your minds together.
Charlie No, I mean — bored when the act finished. The performing is what held us together. We were a team. We argued, we clashed, but when the lights came up, we had to get on with it. Yes, it was when the curtain dropped — that's what did it. There's nothing worse than a performer without a stage. We drive everybody nuts — don't we, Jack?
Jack You certainly do!
Maggie Don't tell him that! God, you're as sensitive as a brick.
Jack What's wrong with saying that? It's honest.
Maggie Even *I'm* thinking of leaving the pair of you. Charlie — just talk to her. Tell her you love her. That you'll try and change. No. That you *will* change. You have to give her a reason to try again. If she planned all this — moving the two of you in here — arranging tickets and taxis, secret midnight departures — then she's been thinking about this for a while. It's not spur of the moment, she —— She *means* it. Do you understand?

Charlie gives Maggie a kiss on the cheek

Charlie I'll be in the car.

Charlie exits. Geraldine enters with a huge tray of food

Geraldine This should keep us going.
Jack Are you expecting a *siege* of some kind?
Geraldine Charlie in the car?
Maggie Yes. (*She lays her coat on the tray for her to take with her*)
Geraldine (*to Jack*) We'll do what we can.
Jack Bring her back. Please.

Geraldine nods

Geraldine It'll be several hours. Get some sleep.

She exits

Maggie closes the door

Jack Sleep? I don't think either of us will be able to sleep.
Maggie Actually, I might drop off for a bit.
Jack At a time like this!
Maggie I just broke up with my boyfriend over corned beef hash and lilies. I'm exhausted!
Jack He wasn't your boyfriend. You only went out twice.
Maggie That's very good for me. I was making a special effort.
Jack ... I don't know why any of us bother with relationships. You grow old together and then discover after forty years that you've nothing in common. And yet whether we're single or widower, we pursue this illogical desire to share our bread — and indeed our bed — with some other like-minded soul who will likely leave or die at the most inconsiderate moment. We should all live separate lives in small boxes mounted on hillsides and be content with our lot. I'd much prefer ten good friends. No — four good friends and some colourful acquaintances for decoration. I realize the need for breeding — but really, how many more screaming children do we need? The schools are already full of the blighters and less than half a dozen will make a valuable contribution to society while the rest flick gum into each other's hair and declare how they hate their parents who never give them what they want. Unconditional love being the world's most unappreciated gift. I don't know a single child who wouldn't happily

trade in his parents for a bottle of coke and a bag of crisps. So the having of kids is no excuse to get into the great marital bun fight. Relationships therefore remain completely unnecessary ... Though there's the need for occasional sex, of course, but I'm sure we could invent some machine to take care of that. It would be quicker and cleaner and when you lose interest, you can just stick it in the cupboard.

Maggie And what about having to eat alone? If you're not *with* someone, you're condemned to eat every ghastly meal alone.

Jack Distinctly *under*rated.

Maggie Not so. It's horrible. People stare at me like I have leprosy.

Jack So find a table in a darker corner.

Maggie I want to be in the light. Middle of the room. That's where I've always been. And I'm fed up of eating solo. I've eaten in restaurants my entire career. And even when I was young, gorgeous and poor — I was there eating on my own.

Jack How could you afford it?

Maggie The restaurants near the theatres used to help me out by giving me all their leftovers. My supper was created out of whatever people left on their plates. It was marvellous — I never paid a penny and one was constantly surprised by the combinations. Now when I eat out, I always leave a solitary sausage or bread roll behind. To encourage young talent.

Jack How very charitable.

Maggie I just wish there was a nice gentleman on the other side of the table.

Jack Who has nothing to say.

Maggie He doesn't have to talk. I've often found men's conversation an unhelpful distraction. So long as he's there to pass the mustard and show the world that I am not alone.

Jack Oh, for goodness' sake, woman. I'll eat with you. You only have to ask. (*He sits down beside her on the sofa*)

Maggie Well, that's not the issue.

Jack The odd thing is — you so rarely *do* ask. Why is that?

Maggie I presume you're busy.

Jack Busy!? At midnight?

Maggie Well, I don't want to disappoint Geraldine. She prepares you those lovely suppers. If you stopped coming home after a show, you'd break her heart.

Jack Geraldine's heart is not my concern.

Maggie No, I don't think it's anybody's concern. Poor dear.

Jack If eating alone is such a bind, then we can — whenever you wish — take supper after the shows. You and I. I'll even buy you lilies.

Maggie And if I die one day, I'll accept them.

Jack *If* you die?

Maggie I'm hoping one day they'll invent a machine to do that for us too. (*She smiles. A moment*) ... It'll be all right.

Jack What will?

Maggie *Everything.* Your mum and dad. Me and my dining habits. You and — whatever it is you want ... And what do you want these days, my darling? Are you still not ready to be romanced? At some point, you'll have to at least open yourself up to the idea.

Jack I don't see why I should.

Maggie People do, Jack. They mend themselves and then they start moving forward again. One step at a time.

Jack I'm not ready.

Maggie Oh, my dear, you'll never be ready. It doesn't work as simply as that. I think there just reaches a moment when you take a blind leap. Dive into the shallow swimming pool.

Jack And break your neck.

Maggie Very possibly. But you can't avoid it forever. You can't *mourn* forever.

Jack Why not? In Spain they do. When a woman loses her husband, she wears black — only black — for the rest of her life. The streets are filled with these colourless elderly women whose lives have just suddenly stopped.

Maggie Yes and who want to make damn sure we know it. I mean I'm all for a little bit of mourning, but why take it out on the rest of us? Any widowed *men* — I presume — can go back to tropical shirts and linen trousers as soon as they fancy?

Jack I presume.

Maggie Now why doesn't that surprise me? I just don't think men love in quite the same way.

Jack We do our best.

Maggie You did more than your best, Jack. I thought you loved your wife magnificently.

Jack Do you think she noticed? I wish I could just tell her. Just once more — to make sure she knew.

Maggie When my mother died, my father said he would give up everything he had if he could spend just one more day with her. Would you?

Jack No. A day is not enough. I was promised a lifetime.

Maggie Well, nobody keeps promises anymore. I'm sorry to say.

Jack (*after a brief pause*) Are you sure you don't want to at least call him?

Maggie Who?

Jack Roger. I'm sure he deserves a second chance ... Third chance. It can't have been that terrible. He's always perfectly nice to me.

Maggie I don't want a man who's perfectly nice to *you*. He was perfectly *beastly* to me. And that's only forgivable if you're handsome — and even that he can't manage.

Jack Aren't we being a bit choosy? Just twenty years ago, you were licking other people's plates!

Maggie But *he* doesn't know that!

Jack Not till I tell him at the club tomorrow night.

Maggie Oh I can't perform tomorrow. I feel such a fraud. Standing there singing about how love will blossom in the most unexpected ways. We should be thrown in jail.

Jack We sing comic songs as well.

Maggie Yes — and to contemplate falling in love at my age, you really do need a sense of humour.

Jack You're not that old.

Maggie I never said I was "*that* old"!!

Jack (*grimacing*) Sorry.

Maggie I just need a bit of assistance, that's all — a few creams and potions. In Paris you can buy all these concoctions — for your skin, for your complexion. All to reverse the *signs* of growing old. Now if they brought one out that reversed you *actually* growing old, I'd buy the bloody stuff. The signs don't bother me half as much as the ticking clock. Getting louder and louder.

Jack Someone will turn up. "You just have to have faith". That's what they say.

Maggie Who are these people who say these things? I bet they're all single. (*She yawns*) Sorry. I'm even sending myself to sleep these days ... Which is mine?

Jack Which what?

Maggie Bed. I need a bed. Or am I on the couch?

Jack End of the corridor. Anything you want to take with you?

Maggie I'll take anything I can get my hands on. (*Looking at Jack*) Even the unattainable.

Jack I meant a book? Glass of water?

Maggie I know what you meant ... I'll settle for a kiss good-night.

He duly gives her a kiss good-night, as requested. She walks to the door leading to the bedrooms and opens it

Will you be all right on your own?

Jack Perfectly. I'm perfectly used to it.

Maggie gives him a reassuring smile. She exits

A moment. Then Jack walks over to the piano and sits at it. He begins to play (perfectly) the melody that we are about to hear used as the scene change music

As he does so, the Lights fade to black-out. During the scene change, music of the 1950s period is heard — Garland, Astaire, Coward, Sinatra, etc., whatever melody Jack has just played

SCENE 2

The same. The following morning

The room is empty. We hear a car drive up outside and park. Car doors open and close. The front door opens. A suitcase appears first, then revealing Geraldine as she carries it into the room and places it to one side

Geraldine I'll put the kettle on.

She heads downstage and into the kitchen

Beatrice enters. She stands in the doorway surveying the room. She removes her coat and hangs it up

Jack, now fully dressed, emerges from the kitchen. He is carrying a plate of half-eaten cake and has a fork in his other hand

Jack Mum!? Well, thank God! You see now what I've resorted to. You do a thing like that again and I'll have to buy bigger trousers ... Now then ——
Beatrice Don't — don't say anything. I came back, didn't I?
Jack You shouldn't have gone in the first place. Heaven knows what might have happened.
Beatrice Well nothing did happen. So you can finish your breakfast. (*She moves downstage*) Geraldine's making tea.
Jack I know.
Beatrice I would have brought croissants, but I didn't get that far. (*She sits on the sofa*)
Jack And a good job too. All right — let's take stock. I've a lot of questions. But — let's be calm about it. We'll have a drink — and we'll sit down and talk — the three of us.
Beatrice *Two*, dear.

Jack Um?
Beatrice The two of us.
Jack Why? Where's Dad?
Beatrice France.
Jack France!?
Beatrice Why waste the ticket?
Jack Mum!?

Beatrice delivers the following whole speech in almost a single breath

Beatrice Look, Jack, we didn't really need to talk about much — it was perfectly clear we couldn't live together anymore and he said you were beside yourself and I had to come home or you'd have a heart attack. And I said if that meant coming home with you, you could forget it and he said well if that's the way it is we'd have to live in separate houses and I said that's fine but there's no way I was moving out of our home and so that meant he'd have to live with you. And it was obvious that wouldn't work because you'd end up throttling each other. So he suggested that *he* goes to France because he'd never been and I gave him all the francs I had and off he went in search of garlic and can-can girls while I drove back with Geraldine — and it's all turned out rather well if you think about it, though not quite as any of us expected ... Is there any more of that cake?
Jack Take it, I've lost my appetite. (*He gives her his plate of cake*) So what exactly — just explain again ——
Beatrice No, I'm not saying it again, I'll need an oxygen tent.
Jack Dad's in France?
Beatrice Yes, dear.
Jack Where exactly?
Beatrice Well presuming he turns up to meet me at the port like we arranged — he'll be staying with Gypsy Jean Paul.
Jack Rabbit?
Beatrice It's pronounced Rabert.
Jack Won't he be surprised?
Beatrice Yes, I think he will. But I don't see that he can turn him away. He was offering a spare bed — so he'll just have to accommodate.
Jack But wasn't he expecting something ... romantic ..?
Beatrice Oh, don't be ridiculous. I gave up all that bedroom business years ago. Your father and I mutually agreed to bring a halt to all that. It was too time-consuming. I mean I like a nice drive in the country as much as the next girl, but when it takes half an hour to get the car started, you lose interest.
Jack So — hang on — when's he coming back?

Beatrice I don't know — it was a one-way ticket. I expect he'll be gone a while — you know how your dad loves touring.

Jack Has he got enough money?

Beatrice Plenty. I gave him all my French francs, thousands of them. I've been saving for ages — that's why we kept coming here to eat. Eating at your son's house can save you a fortune. I don't know why more parents don't do it. And you never minded, did you dear?

Jack If I'd known what was going on, you wouldn't have got so much as a bread roll. How long have you been planning this?

Beatrice A long time. The situation's been very clear for a long time ... And actually — I think this trip will do Charlie some good. A change of air.

Jack And what about a change of clothes?

Beatrice Hm?

Jack All he took with him was his hat, passport and a cream sponge ...

Beatrice No, I only brought home *one* of the suitcase — he took the other one with him — it's full of clothes.

Jack *Women's* clothes!

Beatrice He's going to *France*, dear, I doubt anyone will notice.

Jack I think I need to sit down. (*He slumps into the armchair*)

Beatrice You poor thing — have you stayed up all night?

Jack Of course I have.

Beatrice And Maggie too?

Jack Of course she hasn't. She's in the spare room, away with the fairies.

Beatrice I am sorry.

Jack No you're not.

Beatrice I am! I just didn't know what else to do. I had to get away — and I had to leave Charlie *with* somebody. So I brought him here before I did anything else. Otherwise he wouldn't have coped.

Jack Why do you care?

Beatrice Because he's my husband.

Jack Who you don't love.

Beatrice Who I *tried* to love. For many, many years. You can fool him, your friends and even an audience, but you can't fool your heart.

Geraldine enters with a tray holding a teapot, cups and saucers

Geraldine I'll pop it on the piano — you can help yourselves.

Jack Thank you, Geraldine. I mean — *thank you.*

Geraldine My pleasure. Do you mind if I — go to bed?

Jack No — please. And make tomorrow a day off.

Geraldine Oh — thank you. I'll take myself away on a trip somewhere.

Jack I hear France is lovely ..!

Geraldine I think I'll stay closer to home. (*To Beatrice*) As we all should ..? Good-night ... well — good-morning.

She exits through the kitchen

Beatrice She's rather wonderful, isn't she.
Jack Yes — I couldn't manage without her. She's saved the day on many occasions. Not just today ... And in those months after Alison died, she — well ... She saved my life.
Beatrice But it doesn't need saving any more, does it?
Jack I don't know.

Beatrice looks at him

No, I suppose not. Not anymore.
Beatrice Then you should start looking again.
Jack Mum ... I don't think you're the one to give me advice on matters of the heart.
Beatrice I'm not. But let me just say this — one step at a time. I'm not saying there's any rush. You could start by releasing Geraldine. Cut her chains. Let her run off to some other spoiled theatrical.
Jack And who would butter my toast?
Beatrice Maggie?
Jack Maggie? That relationship is strictly professional.
Beatrice I don't think she sees it that way. I don't think she ever has.
Jack Mother —
Beatrice I'll pour the tea. (*She heads to the piano where she will proceed to pour two cups of tea as they talk*)
Jack If any relationship should be under discussion — it's yours.
Beatrice No. I'm not going to talk about it. You know perfectly well what a nightmare your father is — and you are not going to fool me into thinking you don't understand completely why I left. So let's not have another word about it. I'm here with the tea and he's there wearing one of my old frocks — and that's that.

Jack gets up and crosses to her

Jack You know why this went wrong? You stopped performing. The two of you should never have stopped performing.
Beatrice Jack — there wasn't any work.
Jack So take a show to old people's homes, children's parties, fêtes, festivals. You could have even done a turn each Saturday night with me at the Café de Paris. I'm just saying — if you'd carried on performing, the marriage might well have survived a lot better.

Beatrice But on what terms? If you need braces and wig tape to hold a marriage together, what good is it? (*She adds milk to the tea*)

Jack I just don't want all of us to end this life single.

Beatrice Single is not half as bad as it's said to be.

Jack How would you know — you've only been single for six hours. You might want to give it twenty-four before drawing any conclusions.

Beatrice Drink your tea.

Jack I'm worried about Dad.

Beatrice Don't be — he makes friends very easily. He'll probably be around the ship's piano right now, singing out the old songs for free beers. He'll have an audience there and wherever he goes. That's all he needs. And good luck to him. He always loved an audience more than he loved me.

Jack Mum —

Beatrice No — I'm glad of it. He loved them and they loved him back. *That* was the perfect relationship ... Cheers. (*She holds up her tea cup*)

Jack does nothing, so Beatrice just chinks her cup against his. Then she heads back to sit on the sofa

Do you have a show tonight?

Jack Yes, we do.

Beatrice Can I come?

Jack Providing you leave your passport here — yes.

Beatrice ... You know, it's odd — I'm glad to be home. I mean a foreign adventure with a French gypsy is all very well, but it doesn't beat a nice cup of tea, does it?

Jack I don't know how you can be so calm about everything. You throw everyone's life into turmoil and then you settle down with a pot of Earl Grey as though nothing's happened.

Beatrice What do you want me to do? Burst into tears? Throw myself on a funeral pyre?

Jack No, but perhaps you could just *feel* something.

Beatrice I am not heartless — far from it. I just don't think we have to handle everything hysterically. I had enough of that in the theatres. Shouting, screaming, slamming doors. People threatening to kill each other. And the next day, they're all cuddling and falling about together like a couple of puppies. I am going to handle the entire remainder of my life on a flat platform, an even keel. Calm and tranquillity, peace and quiet. Everything polite and friendly. Now shut up and drink your tea!

Jack Don't you talk to me like that — I am not your husband. And after today — *you* don't get to give anybody instructions.

Beatrice I'm not instructing, Jack, I'm *pleading*. Please — let's just have five minutes ..?

Jack agrees to this and sits next to Beatrice on the sofa. They drink their tea in silence. A few moments pass, then the doorbell rings

Jack Geraldine will get it.
Beatrice You sent Geraldine to bed. The poor lass had to drive all the way to Dover.

Beatrice drinks her tea as Jack stares at her in disbelief. He then gets up, hands her his cup, and walks to the door

Jack opens the door and — to his great surprise — Charlie enters. He strides immediately to centre stage. He is wearing a blue and white striped polo shirt, a beret, and has a string of onions hanging around his neck

Jack Dad!?

Beatrice stands up, shocked

Beatrice Charlie!?
Jack But —— How did you get back so quick?
Charlie Jumped off the ship before it even left.
Jack So — where did you get the bloody outfit?
Charlie Souvenir shop, Dover.
Jack And the onions?
Charlie Greengrocers, Canterbury.
Beatrice Charlie! Why have you come back? I thought we ——
Charlie I know, I know. But you've always loved surprises, haven't you?
Beatrice I'm starting to go off them.
Charlie I couldn't just sail away from everything — even if there was a tanned gypsy awaiting me at the other end. I belong *here*. We belong together — Charlie and Beat — just like it said on all those theatre posters.
Beatrice Those theatre posters were torn up a decade ago.
Charlie But this marriage wasn't. We're still breathing — well, coughing and wheezing. Look, Beat, I've been thinking about everything and — well, I have a suggestion ... How about you stay in our house and we'll buy a car and a caravan — and I'll spend my week travelling the country. I love being out on the road. And you can have the peace and

quiet you want. I'll just come home at the weekend — and by then, you might miss me ... Does that sound a good idea?

Beatrice Is that something you'd really want to do?

Charlie Yes, I'd love it. Visiting all the old towns, the old theatres every week. I can't think of anything better.

Beatrice Then why didn't you suggest it before?!

Charlie I thought you couldn't live without me! But now I realize you can't live *with* me. I'm always getting things muddled ... We can still be happy, can't we? I just thought that maybe if we were always apart — that would mean we could stay together. If you see what I mean?

Beatrice Well, I ... I suppose it's something that *might* work. I'll have to think about it.

Jack I have another thought to add. If you come back each weekend, to be together, then why don't you perform with me — every Saturday, at the Café de Paris. You'd have your own lives, separate, apart — however you want it — but every weekend we'd be there together. The Nightingale family, singing together at night the way nightingales are designed to do. It would be — well, it *could* be — wonderful. You'd be performing again. And we'd be there, all of us as a family, doing my show. Me and Maggie doing our usual set, but with an added bonus of "Charlie and Beat" as our supporting act.

Beatrice I'm sorry — "supporting" act?!

Jack All right — shared billing. We can discuss it with my agent.

Beatrice I thought he was dead.

Jack Only from the neck upwards.

Charlie What do you say, Beat? I go off on my travels and then once a week we get together on stage?

Beatrice I don't know. I mean — what kind of marriage is that?

Charlie *Unconventional* — the kind that works.

Beatrice But isn't this all just ——

Jack I know, I know, let's just — let it roll around in our heads for a while. Let's just — have a cup of tea.

Jack and Beatrice retrieve their cups of tea and Charlie goes to the piano to pour one for himself

Maggie enters from the bedrooms

Maggie Oh! You're all back.

Charlie We never left — you must have had a nightmare.

Jack We're having tea. Can I get you a cup?

Maggie Someone tell me I'm not going mad.

Jack I can't do that, I'm not a medical professional. And your head does often turn to marmalade.

Maggie Jack — will you just tell me ——
Jack No. Some other time. For now, let's just —— (*To Charlie*) Milk and two sugars for Maggie please, Dad.

Maggie approaches Charlie who makes her a cup of tea. At this moment, Geraldine enters in her nightclothes

Geraldine Can someone please tell me what's going on?
Jack
Beatrice } (*together*) We're having tea.
Charlie
Maggie

Geraldine walks to the piano and each finishes adding milk and sugar to their cup of tea and they gather in various seats in the front room, except for Geraldine who remains standing. They drink their tea, saying nothing. After a moment, Jack breaks the silence

Jack I always dreamed that I would again one day sit in silence in my living-room. It's wonderful.

The silence continues for a moment

Good — now that's over with — Geraldine, put the radio on, would you?

Geraldine switches on the radio. It loudly plays Bill Haley's "Rock Around the Clock". They sit listening to it, reacting with horror and grimacing at the sounds they are hearing. Geraldine however nods her head to the music. After about half a minute, Jack signals for Geraldine to switch the volume off. She does so

Charlie What was that?!
Jack I think that was our funeral ...
Geraldine Shall I search for another channel? Find something a bit more "yesterday"?
Maggie (*to Jack*) Is that what we are — *yesterday*?

Geraldine changes the radio channel and settles on Frank Sinatra singing "In the Wee Small Hours of the Morning". There is an audible sigh of relief and they continue drinking their tea with smiles of contentment. Geraldine lowers the volume and the music continues quietly in the background

Maggie Is somebody going to tell me what happened?

Beatrice It's a long story.

Maggie I'm single and I live alone — take as long as you like.

Charlie You ever been in a caravan?

Maggie No — fate hasn't yet thrown that particular delight at me.

Charlie I'm going to buy one. They're the very latest thing. Modern and mobile. I'm off to travel the country and then come back once a week to appear with you two in your show each Saturday.

Maggie Sorry? Appear with us in the —— ? Jack?

Jack Yes, I have to talk to you about that.

Maggie Yes, I think you do.

Charlie Aren't you pleased?

Maggie (*drily*) Oh — pleased is not the word ... (*She drinks her tea*)

Charlie It'll take a bit of sorting out — but it's something for you to look forward to in the future.

Maggie Oh, Charlie, I try not to think too much about the future. I'm still trying to get through this morning.

Beatrice How is all this going to work exactly?

Charlie We'll talk about it. We'll talk about *everything* ...

Beatrice So talk. I'm listening.

Charlie No, not here. I think we need to go somewhere private.

Beatrice Then let's go home.

Jack (*delighted*) Home!? *Your* home? Really!?

Beatrice Yes, I think that's a good idea. But don't get too excited, Jack — we'll be back for lunch.

Jack Ah ...

Beatrice But we'll take the suitcases with us — all right? Start the process of moving out. Would that make you happy, Jack?

Jack I think I may cry.

Beatrice Help me get up then.

Jack Just one thing first — if you go ahead with all this — don't worry about your savings. I'll pay for the caravan, petrol, the outfits for the show, whatever else you need.

Charlie Pay for it with what?

Jack Money, Dad. I have plenty of it — all saved up for a rainy day. And today we all got drenched.

Charlie We can't take your money.

Jack Oh, nonsense. What are your children for? I'll even give you pocket money. — It's fine. They pay me very well. You're welcome to it. Truly.

Charlie And so they should pay you well. You deserve it.

Jack I do?

Charlie Absolutely you do. That's why I've always been so jealous of you.

Jack (*taken aback*) Jealous of me?
Charlie Yes, son. Why do you think we argue all the time? ... But that's
for another day. (*He stands up. To Beatrice*) Are we going then?
Beatrice I suppose we are.

*Charlie puts out his hand and brings Beatrice to her feet. The music
changes on the radio. It plays Fred Astaire singing "Cheek to Cheek".
A moment*

Charlie Beatrice — I'm not very good at saying sorry, but — instead
— may I have this dance?
Beatrice What dance?

*Charlie gestures for Geraldine to turn up the volume on the radio. She
does so*

Get rid of the vegetables and I'll think about it. You should know by
now I have no interest in your onions.

*Charlie discards his beret and string of onions and then offers himself as
her dance partner. They take each other by the hand and begin to slowly
dance around the room, circling the piano. The others watch them. After
a while, Jack turns to Maggie*

Jack Shall we?
Maggie Before breakfast?
Jack Think of it as very, very late at night.

*The two of them stand and also dance. Both couples circle the piano.
Eventually, Charlie and Beatrice stop dancing and walk towards the
front door. Geraldine lowers the volume of the music*

Beatrice Apology accepted.
Charlie Thank you.
Beatrice Take the case, Charlie.
Geraldine I'll get it for you.
Beatrice No — you'll catch your death in that outfit. Charlie can manage.
Geraldine If you're sure?
Charlie Not a problem.

*Charlie picks up the suitcase, as Beatrice gives Geraldine a grateful
kiss*

Beatrice Thank you.

Beatrice exits

Charlie follows with the suitcase

Jack See you at lunch. — Dad! Make sure that case doesn't hit the ——

At this moment the suitcase slams into the frame of the front door

Charlie It's all right — I've got it.

Charlie exits with the suitcase

The song ends on the radio. Jack and Maggie are still in each other's arms. Geraldine switches off the radio and senses this might be a good time to leave

Geraldine Maybe I'll just go and get dressed — or go back to bed — or ...

Geraldine exits quietly through the kitchen door

Maggie Poor Geraldine — she had nobody to dance with ... She never does.
Jack But she gets Mondays off, you know. She might be dancing with all kinds of people we don't know about.
Maggie Oh, I think she only has eyes for one person. (*She breaks from Jack and moves down to sit on the sofa*) You know, if you ever cease her employment — I don't think she'll have anywhere to go. There aren't many theatrical bachelors left any more. You're a dying breed. I'm quite sure you'll be the last of her "gentlemen".
Jack Why would I ever let her go?
Maggie You might get married.

Jack sits next to her on the sofa

Jack To whom exactly?
Maggie Some secret admirer. Someone who understands you — adores you ... Someone — who'll make you learn to cook.
Jack Cook?
Maggie You've a very expensive kitchen out there — just along the corridor. You should go find it — I'll draw you a map.
Jack Traditionally, I believe the woman does the cooking.

Maggie laughs

Maggie Oh, you are funny ..! You realize we're going to have to find new songs for the show. We're going to have to pull all the stops out if your parents are going to be stealing our thunder every night.

Jack Only on Saturdays.

Maggie I shouldn't have to put up with it. I shall be speaking to my agent.

Jack If he remembers who you are — then good luck to you. Can I have my breakfast now?

Maggie Yes, I suppose — just give me a quick kiss first.

Jack gives her a quick peck on the lips

Jack Do you think everything will be all right?

Maggie Most things are — in the end.

Jack It has always amazed me that things don't get easier as you get older. Love, relationships, marriage. It just seems whatever stage you are in life, love is always a steep climb uphill.

Maggie Yes — but if you get to the top — it's a lovely view.

Jack And how would you know?

Maggie Oh I know a great deal about relationships. I've had *hundreds* of them ..! (*She looks at Jack*) But never the one I've always wanted.

Jack (*after a brief pause*) I know ... Just give me time.

Maggie I don't think there is much time any more, Jack. It's going out of fashion terribly quickly.

Maggie gets up and wanders slowly across the room

Jack Where are you going?

Maggie I thought I might explore the kitchen. In case one day we need to learn to cook in it. (*She pauses at the kitchen door*) ... Shall we attempt scrambled eggs?

Jack I think that's a *terrible* idea.

Nonetheless, Jack gets up and heads towards the kitchen. They smile at each other. Maggie giggles. She reaches out her hand to lead Jack into the kitchen. She moves through the door, but Jack stays by the doorway and pulls her back out again

Maggie I thought we were ——

Jack brings her close and kisses her — passionately, but gently

But what about your breakfast?

Jack Oh, to hell with my breakfast!

They kiss again. Music rises in the background — the final moments of a romantic song of the period, ideally something heard earlier in the show

The Lights fade to black-out as the song ends

CURTAIN

FURNITURE AND PROPERTY LIST

ACT I

SCENE 1

On stage: Piano. *On it*: spectacles (for **Jack**)
Armchairs
Sofas
Tables. *On one of the tables*: cups, plates, milk, sugar,
    empty biscuit jar, pot of tea
Drinks cabinet. *On it*: liqueur decanter, brandy decanter,
    whisky bottle, gin bottle, glasses
Small cabinet containing sherry bottle
Telephone
Coat stand. *On it*: scarf
Corner lamp
Lamp
Radio
Tea cup (for **Maggie**)
Pen (for **Maggie**)
Plate. *On it*: large chocolate biscuit (for **Maggie**)
Hooks. *On them*: **Maggie**'s fur coat, keys
Contracts (in **Maggie**'s coat pocket)

Off stage: Pot of jam (**Charlie**)
Porter's trolley, huge trunk containing dust and debris, comedy
    spectacles with giant eyeballs on coils, two British flags,
    bottle of whisky, stupid hat, false moustache, small flute
Two large suitcases (**Charlie**)
Two large suitcases (**Geraldine**)
Damp cloth (**Geraldine**)
Damp cloth (**Beatrice**)
Handful of letters including a pink envelope
    (**Stage Management**)
Trays of breakfast foods including plates, cups, coffee,
    sandwiches and napkins (**Geraldine** and **Maggie**)

Personal: **Jack**: watch

SCENE 2

On stage: As before

Off stage: Two suitcases (**Beatrice**)
                Rolling pin, large whisk (**Geraldine**)
                Bedraggled bunch of lilies (**Maggie**)
                Note (**Charlie**)

ACT II

SCENE 1

On stage: As before

Off stage: Bag stuffed with a few items (**Charlie**)
                Huge tray of food (**Geraldine**)

SCENE 2

On stage: As before

Off stage: Suitcase (**Beatrice**)
                Plate of half-eaten cake, fork (**Jack**)
                Tray holding tea pot, cups and saucers (**Geraldine**)

LIGHTING PLOT

Property fittings required: corner lamp, lamp
Interior, the same throughout.

ACT I, SCENE 1

To open: General interior lighting

Cue 1	**Jack** finishes playing the tune *Fade Lights to black-out*	(Page 24)

ACT I, SCENE 2

To open: Moonlight and corner lamp

Cue 2	Beatrice is halfway to the front door *Light from bedrooms* L	(Page 25)
Cue 3	**Geraldine** turns room lights on *Bring up Lights*	(Page 26)
Cue 4	**Beatrice**: "I can't ... I can't ..." *Headlights shine through window*	(Page 28)
Cue 5	**Maggie**: "Isn't there any sherry?" *Headlights move off window as car drives away*	(Page 28)
Cue 6	**Jack**: "Oh, Maggie." *Headlights shine through window*	(Page 31)
Cue 7	**Maggie**: "... and not an inch of progress." *Headlights move off window as car drives away*	(Page 32)
Cue 8	*La Mer* begins to play *Fade Lights very slowly fade to black-out*	(Page 33)

ACT II, SCENE 1

To open: Darkness

Cue 9	*La Mer* plays again *Bring up Lights slowly*	(Page 24)

| *Cue* 10 | **Jack** plays the piano | (Page 42) |
| | *Fade Lights to black-out* | |

ACT II, SCENE 2

To open: General interior lighting

| *Cue* 11 | Music rises in the background | (Page 54) |
| | *Fade Lights to black-out* | |

EFFECTS PLOT

ACT I

Cue 1   To open ACT I, SCENE 1   (Page 1)
A song of the 1950s plays, then fades

Cue 2   **Maggie** heads towards the UC door   (Page 5)
Doorbell rings

Cue 3   **Geraldine**: "... everybody loves me."   (Page 13)
Doorbell rings

Cue 4   Lights fade to black-out   (Page 24)
Music of the 1950s plays during the scene change

Cue 5   **Beatrice**: "... I can't ... I can't ..."   (Page 28)
A taxi pulls up outside

Cue 6   **Maggie**: "Isn't there any sherry?"   (Page 28)
The taxi drives off

Cue 7   **Jack**: "Oh, Maggie."   (Page 31)
Another car pulls up outside

Cue 8   **Maggie**: "Three dates and not an inch of progress."   (Page 32)
The car drives off

Cue 9   **Charlie**: "... she thinks of everything ..."   (Page 33)
"La Mer" plays

ACT II

Cue 10   To open ACT II, SCENE 1   (Page 34)
"La Mer" plays, then fades out

Cue 11   Lights fade   (Page 42)
Music of the 1950s plays

Cue 12   To open ACT II, SCENE 2   (Page 42)
A car drives up outside and parks

Cue 13	**Jack** and **Beatrice** drink their tea. Pause *Doorbell rings*	(Page 47)
Cue 14	**Geraldine** switches on the radio *"Rock Around the Clock" by Bill Haley plays*	(Page 49)
Cue 15	**Geraldine** switches the volume off *"Rock Around the Clock" stops*	(Page 49)
Cue 16	**Geraldine** changes the radio channel *"In the Wee Small Hours of the Morning" by Frank* *Sinatra plays*	(Page 49)
Cue 17	**Geraldine** lowers the volume *Music volume decreases*	(Page 49)
Cue 18	**Charlie** brings **Beatrice** to her feet *"Cheek to Cheek" Fred Astaire version plays*	(Page 51)
Cue 19	**Geraldine** turns up the volume on the radio *Music volume increases*	(Page 51)
Cue 20	**Geraldine** lowers the volume *Music volume decreases*	(Page 51)
Cue 21	**Geraldine** switches radio off *Radio off*	(Page 52)
Cue 22	**Jack** and **Maggie** kiss again *Music of the period rises in the background*	(Page 54)

USE OF COPYRIGHT MUSIC

Lightning Source UK Ltd.
Milton Keynes UK
UKHW02f2349230618
324656UK00006B/227/P